THE LOVE LIFE OF BUS SHELTERS

K V SKENE

Cinnamon Press
:: small miracles from distinctive voices ::

Published by Cinnamon Press
Meirion House
Tanygrisiau
Blaenau Ffestiniog
Gwynedd, LL41 3SU
www.cinnamonpress.com

The right of K.V. Skene to be identified as author of this work has been asserted by her in accordance with the Copyright, Designs and Patent Act, 1988. Copyright © 2019 K.V. Skene.
ISBN: 978-1-78864-062-6
British Library Cataloguing in Publication Data. A CIP record for this book can be obtained from the British Library.
All rights reserved. No part of this publication may be reproduced, stored in a retrieval system, or transmitted in any form or by any means, electronic, mechanical, photocopying, recording or otherwise without the prior written permission of the publishers. This book may not be lent, hired out, resold or otherwise disposed of by way of trade in any form of binding or cover other than that in which it is published, without the prior consent of the publishers.
Designed and typeset in Palatino by Cinnamon Press.
Cover design by Jan Fortune. Printed in Poland
Cinnamon Press is represented in the UK by Inpress Ltd and in Wales by the Welsh Books Council

Acknowledgements

With thanks to the editors of journals in which the poems have previously: *The Antigonish Review; The Envoy; Fin; Frogmore Papers; iota; Moodswing; The Nail; New Frontier School Board The New Writer; On the Bus*, Oxford Brookes Poetry Centre; *Penniless Press; Poetry Cornwall; Poetry Nottingham; QWERTY; Southlight & Weyfarers.*

Contents

The Full Life of Houses	7
The Subversive Life of Schools	8
The Beautiful Life of Gyms	9
The Social Life of Computers	10
The CCTV Life of Streets and Shopping Malls	11
The Shelf Life of Supermarkets	12
The Real Life of Office Towers	13
The Half Life of Hotels	14
The Still Life of Parking Lots	15
The Religious Life of Banks	16
The Occasional Life of Churches	17
The Postmodern Life of Museums	18
The Closet Life of Galleries	19
The Dangerous Life of Libraries	20
The Private Life of Parks	21
The Radical Life of Restaurants	22
The Love Life of Bus Shelters	23
The On-again-off-again Life of Buses	24
The Covert Life of Constructions Sites	25
The Virtual Life of Traffic Cones	26
The Passing Life of Post Offices	27
The High Life of Hospitals	28
The Get-a-life of Cemeteries	29
The Unparalleled Life of Trains	30
The Double Life of Airports	31
The Capital Life of Cities	32

For Christopher, Florida, Samantha and Beryl,
for Allyson and Martin,
and always
for Leigh

The Love Life of Bus Shelters

The Full Life of Houses

Windows grant sly glimpses,
spy the slow dance
of awakening rooms as doors
burst, disgorge children,
macs and book bags
the way it should be,
      could be
every single morning
if
only ...
and the happy hellos and goodbyes —
that's the best of it,
the joy,
the catch in the throat.

The Subversive Life of Schools

As you relish the taste and smell
of chalk dust, packed lunches, wet wool,
the thinned-skinned smugness
of a monitor,
you're told something you know is
so wrong so
absolute
it rules out ordinary behaviour, it rules out
'ought' and 'must' and 'should'
and the coherence of this world
pulls apart,
what is 'mine' and 'yours' and 'ours'
follows—
one embarrassing hiccup on the heels of another.

The Beautiful Life of Gyms

Straight into the first solitary slow-pulls,
the cross-trainer, the rower, the heavyweight
burn in your arms, cramp
in your left leg and the heartpound
as you breathe out the pain
over the treadmill's 10k down
to the slow unwinding
and that long hot shower. This hour,
this exhaustion, this
is how you begin, is
what your body tells you, why
your mother told you
Il faut souffrir pour être belle
and you know it's true.

The Social Life of Computers

Just out of hibernation and you're downloading
another search engine and into chat rooms
all over the www and just in time too—
what with the wormholes, the spam, the cookies,
the hackers hoping to justify
their deserts. Just because
you've logged on before
doesn't mean you can't crash
and burn—just the same,
don't get too intimate, don't confess—
not just yet—nor interface
face to face
just in case this virtual identity
isn't.

The CCTV Life of Streets and Shopping Malls

Crossing the street, she stalks
out of range, into
another story, followed by a teen
tottering on uncertain stilettos,
a tall man with a cane, a huddle of hoodies,
the usual dogwalkers and drunks
whose uncertain sins, petty abuses,
occasional embarrassments
should have been too gauche,
too absurd, too intrusive too
1984-ish
to overlook —
they are no more nor less innocent
than everyone else we're currently watching.

The Shelf Life of Supermarkets

Think aubergine, beetroot, cabbage,
        banana, apple.
Think chicken legs, lamb chops, calamari,
        cornflakes, Kleenex.
Think water, wine, whiskey. Think
whatever you want
           now
scan aisle 24,
      35,
      46,
          find yourself at the end
of the line. Think
credit card, club card, coupon, cash. Think
checkout.

The Real Life of Office Towers

All the glass and glare of an ordinary Monday
abandoned by certainty,
the city
absorbs the evening exodus,
grabs you by the scruff
and gives back nothing,
  nothing but
the slight shiver of your reflection—
empty,
empty
choices have been made that you had nothing to do with,
crimes have been committed,
  have been shredded and are already
unreadable.

The Half Life of Hotels

Do Not Disturb—the window's
high and oversees
the parking lot and a skip
in limbo.
There's a reason for rootlessness,
      a reason you are here
                    now
and the ache of anticipation, the
after
taste
of a careless childhood
when you held someone you loved
and the city around you
insisted there'd be a tomorrow.

The Still Life of Parking Lots

Row after row after row after
dawn to dusk to
the graveyard shift.
All styles and sizes and costs and colours and
sun-scorched or splattered or shat upon
out of suburbia, out
of habit ... everywhere
deep pockets are taken for granted
trains are not fashionable,
buses are not ...
and taxies are out of sight
out of choice
bumper to bumper to bumper to
pay and display.

The Religious Life of Banks

Columns, cornices of darkpolished wood
and gleaming bronze stanchions, roped with red velvet,
glide across grey marble toward an impossible window
leaking little light. A hole-in-the-wall
is insufficient if you are to become a serious
seeker. Face your double-breasted god
with gravitas—at one with savings, investments,
mortgages, pensions, loans. It is imperative
you offer up at least three kinds of identification
(plus a copy of your last will and testament).
After a multitude of minions collate signatures
and all documentation is deemed acceptable upstairs,
you may be granted an indulgence—
failure to keep up repayments may result in default, disgrace and/or eternal damnation.

The Occasional Life of Churches

Each window shines with evensong
and small candles burn
in prayer, in the certainty of
Sundays, high days, holy days,
another long march down the aisle,
that old god-scented
story.
There's so much I don't know, can't tell —
forgive
me
whoever locked our souls in — how
continuously we die, how
unbelievable
not to be born.

The Postmodern Life of Museums

Histories/legends/tall tales, eviscerated
and hermetically sealed, appropriate a guise
of wisdom/knowledge/mythology—artefacts
out of another time/place
reincarnate for the casual visitor/
up-market tourist/bored schoolchild. Once
something to be treasured/
            used/
                  stolen/broken/thrown
away. Today no one questions the reconditioned air,
the computer-generated whispers of dead men/
women and their all-important war/
peacemaking. Under shadowless light
our old lie unburied.

The Closet Life of Galleries

Not oil/watercolour/ink on paper/board/
stretched canvas. Not
a collage/construct/sculpture. Not
subjective,
but a connective, coherent patterning
that triggers
even more elaborate and idiosyncratic creations
and, as the craving grows,
anything on the wall, spotlit on shelves,
not compelling, not
addictive, not an irresistible invitation to madness
to the obsessive-compulsive, not the ultimate high
is 'out',
is not excessive enough for the 'in' scene.

The Dangerous Life of Libraries

Shush. There are subversive thoughts
squatting all over these shelves. We are here
for the same reason and for that reason
ask no awkward questions,
accept all theories
as the truth, the whole truth
and nothing but—climate controlled,
computerised, verified to the last Dewey
decimal: birth, infancy, childhood,
puberty (sexual adventuring) maturity, ageing, death
are of taxonomic interest, a kind of
nihilistic progression—neither
happy nor sad.
It's too bad about love.

The Private Life of Parks

Styrofoam cups, cigarette butts, beer cans, bottles,
one soiled sneaker, used condom,
an old man sodden with sleep, the occasional
lover, jogger, rollerblader
and a kid on a scooter
follows the leader,
        keeps up
as best he can and please
don't
walk
on the grass, pick flowers, spit, litter,
let your pet foul the path. Cycles
are forbidden
(whether ridden or not).

The Radical Life of Restaurants

An occasion of white damask, mirrored
silverware, long-stemmed
wineglasses under flattering candlelight
and hunger starts
at the sigh of a grand piano, set aside
after so many years and the waiter,
discretely invisible,
proffers heavily embossed menus,
the finest imaginable appetisers, aphrodisiacs—
a taste of sex—nourishment
an afterthought perhaps *A jug of wine,*
a loaf of bread—and thou ...
inside me
the incredible sadness of satiety.

The Rubaiyat by Omar Khayyam
Translated by Edward J. Fitzgerald 1859

The Love Life of Bus Shelters

Shoulderblade to clavicle, our faces mouldy
as old cheese
long past its sell-by date, the storm
gutter bubbles
black ink when a billboard
               smiles
               down
a brilliant, total, toothpaste smile
and
then …
This is the place, the only place
the episodically embarrassed
can fall into all kinds of love
none the wiser.

The On-again-off-again Life of Buses

It's always the same
hours crawl, inconsequential
as the streets fill
        empty
and the faces at each stop
wear their everydayness
everyday
        it's the slow lane
coming, going
the traffic's predictably
unpredictable
till the end of the line
        till arbitrarily assigned
'Out of Service'.

The Covert Life of Construction Sites

After the rollover years, age
becomes weigh and people labour under it,
take over the school, the park
the playing field, back alley,
wasteground
where bodies are found,
 not found
under a scree of stars,
 CCTV cameras
bent out of shape as yesterday
deconstructs
and tomorrow is built behind hoardings,
out of sight, out
of indifference.

The Virtual Life of Traffic Cones

Pure chance
can't hack it, the thrill
of setting up here, of
diverting, of decamping
overnight
as if the sole reason
for being
lies in-between
gridlock
and chaos and systemically
subverting the ongoing—
as if to be right
or not to be left
is enough.

The Passing Life of Post Offices

Heavy-armed queues push bubble
envelopes, duct taped boxes, mailing
tubes over the counter
to be stamped and sorted and
neither snow nor rain nor heat nor
gloom of night ...
                                  landslides of letters
awaiting divergent delivery lie
one atop the other—ink on pink ribboned
notepaper, blue airmail stationary, watermarked
white bond and birthday/anniversary/Christmas
cards, utility bills, bank statements, wedding
invitations, 'Dear Johns' for prospective exes
primed to explode mail boxes etc ...

The High Life of Hospitals

Immediately after the adrenalin rush,
the speeding ambulance you hit
a blur of doctors and nurses as the doors open
at A&E and the stink
of blood and vomit and disinfectant
and a barrage of surround-sound
winds you down random corridors
as a voice demands name/address/
next of kin
and the curtains close
around you and the pain—then
the slow, gentle needle
that leaves only a drop of blood
and oblivion.

The Get-a-life of Cemeteries

Mourners always drift back to where they came from.
Never mind, behind every stone
a shadow, over every mausoleum
an angel and there's another funeral
and another—not the last—
never that ...
           so we all fall from flesh to ash to dust
to spirit and spirit is us
although unlooked-for. Better
to be mindful than unaware, better
to be mad than sad,
to be alive—not dead after all—
dans le beau de l'air du soir
and that is how we leave you when we must.

The Unparalleled Life of Trains

Ignore the scruffy station, the sub-teens
pseudo suicidal dash, trust
in dumb luck and a schedule
so skewed constant commuters
shrug off derailments
occasioned by sad stupidities at level crossings,
signal failures and/
or the wrong kind of weather and
given *le mot juste*
talk each incident to death. Yet
the 9:05 arrives more or less on time
(as usual) and a few longsuffering souls
disembark (as usual) and
we're all aboard before it rolls away.

The Double Life of Airports

From check-in through security
to Gate #48—this
is terminal territory—the walls
exhale the infectious fetor of exasperated boredom.
This is a where the heart beats too slowly,
where walleyed windows expose ephemeral ideologies
to a flat grey sky
and theories proliferate
on the identity/techniques/whereabouts
of an enemy
and time is annihilated
somewhere between Arrivals and Departure
and Duty Free
we are grounded.

The Capital Life of Cities

Still the blinkered beggar, the blind
and backroom deals appear/disappear
the morning after
coercion/confession/crucifixion,
an exhausted line of credit,
CCC rated
junk and Goldilocks bursts another
bubble before too-big-to-fail pundits
break her heart and her bank and her employer
discloses/forecloses/relocates
to where the labour's greenest/taxes
sweetest; before there are so many voices
singing *Good Night Ladies*
even the bottom feeders clock the exits.

Lightning Source UK Ltd.
Milton Keynes UK
UKHW042320050219